IAN GOUGE

AFTER THE REHEARSALS

First published in paperback format by
Coverstory books, 2018

ISBN 978-1-9997840-5-8

Copyright © Ian Gouge 2018

The right of Ian Gouge to be identified as the author of this work has been asserted by them in accordance with the Copyright, Designs and Patents Act 1988.

All characters and events in this publication, other than those clearly in the public domain, are fictitious and any resemblance to real persons, living or dead, is purely coincidental.

All rights reserved.

No part of this publication may be reproduced, circulated, stored in a system from which it can be retrieved, or transmitted in any form without the prior permission in writing of the publisher.

www.coverstorybooks.com

Other Books by Ian Gouge

Novels and Novellas

An Infinity of Mirrors - Coverstory books, 2018
Losing Moby Dick and Other Stories - Coverstory books, 2017
Losing Moby Dick - Kindle 2015
Writing to Gisella - Kindle 2015
Riding the Escalators - Kindle 2015
The Big Frog Theory - Paperback, 2017; Kindle, 2012

Short Stories

Degrees of Separation - Coverstory books, 2018
Secrets & Wisdom - Coverstory books, 2017

Poetry

Punctuations from History - Coverstory books, 2018
Human Archaeology - Paperback, 2017
Collected Poems (1979-2016) - Paperback, 2017; Kindle, 2018

"Act One"

Jukebox	9
Christmas in Ambleside	11
The Audition	12
Insight	15
Dividing Lines	16
The Time to Choose	20
And all the while…	23
Curtain Call	25
In the Sensory Garden	27
Coming Together	30
After Ethereal Flying	31
Candles	34
Petit Fours	37
A Fair Exchange	40
"They do not move."	42
Release	45

"Act Two"

The Ferryman	49
The Guy most likely to…	50
Take no photographs, but be in many	53
Saltburn	57
Departure	61
The Garden Bench	63
No longer the smell of small miracles	68
For the Love of Daffodils	69
Returning Home	73
"I heard"	76
Decline, the white flag	79
"What next?"	81
Interlocking	84

"Act Three"

Choice 89
Old Shoots, New Leaves 90
The Coniston Question 94
'No' 96
'Yes' 97
If there was a difference.. 98
Skins 99
As if nothing had happened 102
The Sculptor of Life 104
After the Rehearsals 107
The Library 111

*

Acknowledgements 117

"Act One"

Jukebox

Someone once told him
                        there were two reasons for everything.
He liked to think it would have been Jess,
the Jess he hadn't seen for so long now.

Eyes closed.

It was an effort to get this far.

The doctors had told him he was doing well;
recital of their standard patter.
Reason one: to make him feel better.
Reason two: to make them feel better.
The theory seemed to stand up to scrutiny.

He'd come to cherish these rare drug-induced lucid moments.
His medication offered perhaps two brief daily windows
into his past, his life;
if he were lucky, there might be three.
If he were *really* lucky they'd upgrade the dose.

Once upon a time he had been unstoppable
      - whatever that meant.

The drugs allowed him to recreate himself,
to walk again the streets of Sienna or Split,
to take the train all the way to Basel.

From somewhere indistinct yet strangely familiar,
an image of the Styx Ferryman.
He tried to wave it away with a fluttering of his eyelashes.

Two reasons.
It seemed like a new idea, but it couldn't possibly be so;
a universe, one way in, two ways out?

Starved of music,
this old jukebox could only play the records inside it;
the discs were fragments of his past.

All he could do was slide an imaginary coin into the machine
and see what played next.

Suddenly it felt like heaven.

Christmas in Ambleside

At the last minute
they managed to find a minuscule cottage to rent,
crammed into the middle of a small Ambleside terrace,
and when the weather allowed
spent days wrapped up against bitter winds
walking the hills.
In the evenings they huddled by the fire,
watched re-runs of old movies on the ageing television
and struggled with inadequate wi-fi.
They told each other it didn't matter.
It was 'romantic'.
Without saying as much,
they placed apostrophes around the word.

Although he had no idea what it was supposed to feel like -
Christmas, their intimacy, their unspoken routines,
even the way she seemed to know when he needed coffee
or just some time to himself to read -
it felt like growing up,
as if that was how adults were supposed to behave.

The Audition

He *never* kissed anyone like that,
        lips-to-lips, tight, chaste.
He saw the surprise in her eyes,
the reaction to a hint of pressure
as if they were heading towards the edge of a cliff.

He threw himself off.

❋

After Ambleside
New Year's Eve parties offered only disquiet,
yet soon enough reunited in their shabby-chic flat
over the Indian fabric shop, they would be trying to ignore
the Bollywood-style music permeating the floor
as she struggled with The Wars of the Roses
and he The History Plays.

The holidays were a chance to recalibrate,
for him to anticipate the start of rehearsals
even if they'd all said he was mad to take on 'Godot'.
It was 'sparse'.
        He argued
it would impact his studies less than other plays might.
They all knew *that* would prove a lie.
He had assumed an all-male cast:
Harry as Vladimir;
Rich would suit Lucky - if he could be persuaded
to sacrifice his self-image to play the fool.
The right person for Pozzo was key.

Her appearance at the audition had surprised him.
He'd seen her around;
she was unmissable,
even if a single term was never enough
to roughen the edges of kids just out of school.

"Pozzo," she said. "Obviously."

Why hadn't he seen it himself?

Seamlessly launching into Pozzo's first long scene,
she mimed to perfection the interaction with Lucky,
a man - as dog - tethered by a string.
The small ripple of applause gifted from the rehearsal room
subsided - and in the stillness:

"Why Pozzo?"

By the time she'd walked out, he'd made up his mind
"Lucky. I'll enjoy treating him badly!" she'd said.
Something in the comment, the image it created,
caught him off balance
like a drunk slipping from the pavement.

He took a copy of the play to Ambleside
for Mags to read some of Pozzo's lines.
He needed to hear the words in a woman's voice.
He needed an echo of Rosie.

❀

They had been first to the rehearsal room.
After the others found them,

they were all lost for words.
Then they were just looking at *him*.

Trying to imagine Rosie as Pozzo was impossible, his head filled with other images now.

Insight

"Rehearsals? But why?"

[As if unsupervised, his surprise escaped.
Her playful squeeze on his shoulder corralled it again.]

"Why not? I'm interested in progress.
How's Rosie getting on? Is it working out?"

[He determined to double the guard.]

"Fine.
Some problems in a couple of the scenes with Lucky.
Rich is great, but it's not as funny as it should be.
There might be a chemistry problem."

[It was more alchemy than chemistry, and
Mac was worried Rich had the formula for gold.]

"It's because Rosie's a woman.
The dynamic between Pozzo and Lucky,
it's a man-to-man thing.
It works because they're blokes.
Having Rosie play Pozzo - the jokes need to be different.
That's what makes it interesting."

[She had understood in a way that had passed him by.
She understood as Rosie had understood.
She had seen the potential of having Rosie in the role -
and that it would change something fundamental,
as if it were changing the words themselves.]

Dividing Lines

They moved through rehearsals in pulses;
a spurt of progress, the drag when things proved difficult.
Perhaps it was the heartbeat of the way he worked.
The first read-through felt good,
Harry fitting Vladimir like a glove,
a rough-but-stupid arrogance about him.
It was harder to get Patrick to be as naive as needed,
his raw skill pulling him through - that and Harry's
infectious interpretation forcing the two of them to click.
Beyond comfort, Rich had a certain self-image:
he was used to leading roles, to glamour,
but Lucky was just some dumb animal
that occasionally did party tricks.

"Just humour me, Rich. Ok?"

Of course in the end it did work.
He was able to relate to Rich being so off balance
because of Rosie.

"I'm playing a part that I'm not supposed to play;
that a woman's not supposed to play.
I have most to prove."

She inserted into rehearsals
some minor adjustments to Pozzo's words
- "just to make it work for a woman" -
evidence of a focus and determination that never left her;
being single-minded one of her defining characteristics.

Mac was helpless.

Enslaved as they worked on the play,
Rosie had him on a virtual string
as much as if she were dragging Lucky around the stage.
What right had he to be interested in her anyway
given he and Mags were very much a public item?

It was a question that assaulted him.

But it had begun way back.
In Ambleside when he was thinking about the play
he was really thinking about her.
He believed in the supremacy of 'the Craft',
that theatre had a way of working everything out;
although the play inevitably took over,
it could not make Mac's feelings for Rosie
diminish, or subservient, or simply disappear.
Intimately linked, they managed to sketch out a boundary,
a dividing line like blocking on the stage.
Yet he had needed to draw another line,
one whose crossing promised more dramatic consequences.

He and Mags were still together.

Mac found himself acting in a play of his own
- an unscripted double-hander -
suffering the stage fright of improvisation and
the duplicitousness and peril of ad-lib.
Ambleside had tied a knot between them;
he had felt a big chunk of his life was sorted.
Rosie had scuppered all that,
the seed ironically sewn even before they reached the Lakes.
What happened in January wasn't 'new' at all;
it was the second act in a play where Mac was the male lead.

Rosie knew precisely where she stood
- where he stood.

"There are rules.
Number one; the play comes first.
Until we've finished it's the only thing that counts.
Number two; I really, really like you Mac
- but right now you're Mag's man.
That's a little tough for me, but it's ok for now.
I won't sleep with you while that's how things stand.
Once the play's over, then the game changes;
we each of us will have a decision to make.
And at that point, one, two or three of us will get hurt,
and hopefully two of us will be happy."

Because the focus was on the play,
he was able to talk to Mags about it in a detached way;
if Rosie had screwed up during a rehearsal,
he relayed the awfulness of it to Mags
as if it had been Rich or Patrick or Harry.
It was about understanding where he found himself,
as if he were playing two games of chess simultaneously;
his goal for now not to lose either of them.
He still needed pieces on both boards once 'Godot' was over.

Unwittingly, they both made it hard for him.
There were times with Mags when contentment flooded back,
and he questioned everything he was doing.

"I'm not happy with it. Maybe I should just give it up."
(Of course, by 'it' he said 'Godot' but meant Rosie.)

Mags talked him round.
She knew how important the play was; how he needed it.

Then he and Rosie would edge to their uncrossable line.
Mac would say he had to end things with Mags
and Rosie would harden herself,
tell him he wasn't thinking straight.

"You know this better than most; timing's everything."

The Time to Choose

It was inevitable he would slip somehow,
multiple lives bleeding into each other.
Tutors insisted on greater commitment;
evidence to be more tangible.

"I'm sorry Michael, but your last effort wasn't up to scratch."

He liked Frank and had been told the topic was a breeze,
but Frank could easily spot standard interpretations;
he expected original thinking
      - but original thinking took time.

"It was too short; too derivative.
I can see when it's you, an original thought.
It would have taken Sherlock Holmes at his sharpest
to find either in this last piece.
So what is it? What's the problem?
Burning the candle at both ends?"

"And maybe a little in the middle too…"

This second year was all about self-discovery,
who you were, what you wanted
      - and, in his case, *who* you wanted too.
Nothing academic could give him the buzz
he was getting from "Godot"
      - nor from walking the tightrope
           held, at either end, by Mags and Rosie.

In Mags' kitchen eating toast and drinking tea.
Toast, her favourite thing in the world.

As their relationship matured,
they found time apart was acceptable, essential.
Mac once joked he needed time to recuperate,
but it was more about private space,
to affirm they could still function as individuals.
After heavy "Godot" rehearsals,
Mac needed that separation more and more.

"I've noticed. How tired you are.
A little distant sometimes.
It's the pressure of work on top of the play."

"Burning the candle?"

"Why don't we go away, at Easter?
Like we did at Christmas.
One of those woodland lodge places.
What do you think?"

Here was the first of those breaking points,
a question whose answer wasn't about going away
or taking an out-of-term break;
it was a question that could only be answered
as part of the conclusion, his choice,
                                    heads or tails.

Rosie's assertion that there were decisions ahead
made manifest right here.

"Worth finding out."

It was a ploy to buy him some time,
a commodity in increasingly short supply.

Mac tried to map out the remainder of his term
as if putting it all on paper would help,
as if a column of numbers could make any difference.
Given Frank's undisguised warning,
the harsh reality?
                Not owning enough time.

Compromise of one kind or another was needed;
stop doing some things, spend less time on others.
Less time with Mags,
       less time with Rosie,
              his only options.
And he had not consciously registered until now
there were only four more weeks of term.
His decision point a few days away,
he could see the small and currently opaque window
in which it would have to be made.

He stared at the plan he had just roughed out;
how could any of that bring him equilibrium?
Screwing it up, he threw it in a bin
and headed out of the library for coffee.

And all the while...

He had stumbled into Lent without realising -
not that he had anything to give up;
his belief had never extended that far.

So he abandoned nothing; took more on.
He felt himself becoming the opposite
of what he needed to be,
a mirror image of what others wished to see.

It was the opposite of a Wilderness too,
filled with challenges for a soul
tormented in non-Biblical ways.
There is blankness in the void of a desert,
a shifting repetition in dry sand
blown hard into skin rubbed raw,
into eyes too tearful to see.
The grains on Mac's horizon were of mythic proportions
hitting him hard with Prize Fighter ferocity.
Punch drunk, he reeled from scene to scene.

And all the while they honed the play,
smoothed out the bumps,
perfected their timing 'til it seemed God-given.
Mac watched it go round and round,
a ferris wheel of consummate togetherness,
a culmination of his skill.

And all the while they honed the play
parts of his world succumbed to sand,
crumbling into submission.
Frank shook his head at clumsy depictions;

and Mags ate toast in her kitchen,
alone more often than before.

And all the while they honed the play,
Rosie, shining in his world like a Pole Star
- like *the* star -
moulded his grains of endeavour
into the most solid of blocks,
turned those blocks into a commanding edifice.

And all the while they honed the play
Mac gravitated towards her,
attracted by her presence, her talent;
unable to resist her magnetism,
his was a journey on a narrowing ellipse
knowing there could be no stable orbit.

Curtain Call

The explosion of sound released them all,
dispelling burdens into the air
like dust picked out by stage lights.
They too might have floated away.

From where he stood, watched, paced relentlessly,
standing in the wings, living every line,
he could feel momentum building from the first laugh,
the next overlaid on the last,
layered with pathos,
seasoned with sprinklings of silence,
then racing madly on again towards crescendo.
And they were all brilliant,
Rich and Harry and Patrick:
Rich, who had introduced a nervous tick,
a last-minute idea that by the end
had earned a laugh all its own
like an invisible prompter for the audience,
another character for the play;
Harry, who had become so dishevelled of late;
Patrick, who had redefined perfection
in the way he dovetailed with Harry.

And in the centre of them all,
Rosie's Pozzo dominating;
a presence on the stage
even when she was in the wings.

Mac watched the watchers,
saw them glued to her every move,
pulled taut as if she had them all

attached to Lucky's rope.
Some wanted to swap places with Rich,
to be the unlucky Lucky,
to be bossed and bullied and abused.

And when they called him to the stage,
to accept his share of the encore,
he took part of the audience with him
being tethered to Rosie more than anyone.

Afterwards -
after the laughs, the tears, the hugs,
the friends smuggling themselves backstage
to offer their praise, appreciation,
to be part of the emotion of it all,
to steal a slice of that final scene -
Mac returned to the darkened stage alone,
retrieved the battered shoes
front and centre throughout,
and looked at the front row seat where Mags had sat,
recalling how she had laughed
- and how she had cried at the end.
And even then, in the space about him,
Rosie in possession of everything,
and Mac knowing
Mags would be crying again
                                      soon enough.

In the Sensory Garden

His bedroom felt hollow
as if a thief had stolen in
and removed all that was precious.
An odd sensation, as nothing was missing.
Undisturbed, his books stared back at him;
he could feel their wisdom
    - locked-in secrets camouflaged by language -
        accusing him,
calling him weak, a coward, heartless,
while he, still reeling from the day,
had strived to be everything but.

Not woken by the early morning sun,
greeting the library before it opened
had been easy if out of character;
struggling to concentrate, to read, reorder
others' words, to appropriate them,
to brand them to look like his -
none of that was unusual
    except the spinning in circles,
        the failure to comprehend even the basics,
        anticipation making him dyslexic.

She was waiting for him in the sensory garden,
an award-winning project from way back
when such things were forward-thinking
designed for people who had been robbed
of the taken-for-granted.
It was suddenly an appropriate place,
he dredging himself of the old emotion,
she, nervously trailing her fingers through the lavender,

sensing her world was about to change.

It was over in an instant that seemed to last an eon;
    moments stretched beyond their breaking.
He had never known time could be so elastic.
He tried not to cry
        - then wished he had.
He wanted not to play the card that said
    it was all beyond his control
        - but he did.
He wanted still to be welcome for kitchen toast
        - but knew he never would be.

I knew - she said - something was wrong.
I felt. I saw. I could tell.
But the lack of surprise did not prevent
her being - all the same - surprised.
It did not prevent the tears
or the abuse she hurled his way,
even though she had promised herself
she would not act out of character,
rehearsing the worst-case-scenario
over one extra breakfast slice.

And then she was gone,
the lavender swaying gently in the breeze.

It became a garden devoid of sense
as his room was now devoid of her;
and in his confused attempts
to reconstruct and understand,
he knew that words had done the deed,
and even gifted all the world's words

and the secrets in those books of his,
it was a deed beyond undoing.

Coming Together

Opening the door, she found him
        shrunken, lost, defeated,
and "Poor Mags"
        was the first thing she said.

Then she pulled him in
        as much with her force of will
as the arms that enveloped him,
        that begged him to be still.

Comfort the first thing to offer,
        rousing him, bringing him round,
the rescue of a beached sailor
        whose ship, running aground,

he had abandoned; his life
        left to the fate of the mistress sea,
his body battered, his hopes
        in the wreckage of memory.

After Ethereal Flying

He had not expected theatre,
to be ushered onto a dais defined
by a duvet, floral-patterned, and a bed
sheltered in an arc of flickering tea-lights.
Focussed on her, on the foreignness
of an environment more stage than shelter,
he could hear nothing but his blood,
feel nothing but his blood;
and bound by nothing he could see,
he surrendered to the promise
of a new and magical world sprung
from the folklore of his sacrifice.

Rewarded with a lightness of step,
the rejuvenation of purpose
wiped the grime from the chore of revision
like a windscreen suddenly freed from a distorting frost.
Even Frank, nervous for the final term,
noticed the difference, a return to form.

"This is better, Michael; much more you."

If he attributed the change to the demise of 'Godot'
he did not say
      - but others did,
assuming Mac's rebirth was the manifestation of freedom.

And was it?
Did he ask himself that fundamental question?
Inevitably
      - and inevitably the response

was that his debt was to Rosie.
He was a slave freed from shackles worn so long
had failed to notice them, the chaffing to his skin,
his blood a trail for pursuing hounds.
Having asked himself a question
he assumed a perfect answer,
confusing outcome with evidence.

They breezed through that final term
like carefree seeds surfing an idllic current;
warm in the spring, the heat of summer
lifted them aloft, higher than before.
And while Mac rode the wave,
Rosie played her part
controlling the elements, the ebb and flow,
orchestrating their natural world
as if she were Olympian, all-powerful, invisible.

Did she ask herself if all this was freedom?
Do Gods believe in freedom, the freedom of Man?

❂

Then one day the leaves were suddenly brown.

After their ethereal flying he returned to an autumnal earth,
his buoyancy the camouflage for what couldn't be seen;
deceived by the duplicity of the familiar,
he failed to notice how things had changed.

Rosie's course extracted more from her
and he missed that he was the object
upon which that enforced subtraction worked;

drugged, he missed that as much as he missed
the chasm left by 'Godot'.
Impossibly happy, he failed to recognise
his unresolved feelings for Mags.
He failed to see the leaves
on their journey from green to gold,

Like an actor drunk on success,
seduced by the over-familiarity of a record-breaking run,
he took to the stage anticipating ovations,
the demands for an encore.
In the darkness of the theatre
he failed to see the thinning audience,
failed to hear the indifferent applause,
failed to recognise that at the penultimate curtain call
it was he alone standing in an ever-dimming spotlight.

Then one day the leaves were suddenly brown.

Candles

It was only when she let go of the rope
did he realise he had been tethered.

She, however, had seen it coming all too soon,
recognised the cracks, the fissure ahead,
and as much as she strived to protect what she had
there came a moment, invisible yet distinct,
when self-preservation's call-to-arms
had to be obeyed.

It was game-face time.

That he hadn't seen it coming made it harder.
Suddenly the final act, the denouement's twist,
and while he wasn't looking
(or while he couldn't see)
she blew out the tea-lights
and switched off the spotlight.

❊

Left to the barren darkness of the stage,
he searched for something on which to focus;
yet there was nothing,
> not even a bare tree
> or a pair of battered old boots.

He would have settled for that.

It had been a Friday
> - and in spite of everything Saturday still followed.

He wondered how that could have been possible.

Without recognition or understanding
he collapsed on Sunday,
        internally, invisibly,
and on Monday Frank said lightly

"Heavy weekend?"

"Something like that."

It was as good a description as any other
for he had no idea which words to use.

Now leading on Shakespeare, it seemed as if Frank,
had quietly entered from the darkness of the wings.
His meagre opening line -

"It's time we moved on to 'The Merchant'."

- even though a feeble candle in the gloom,
was at least something to navigate towards.

      "How far that little candle throws his beams!"

❋

He struggled with Antonio
seeing Shylock in the memory of recent faces,
      of others, his own;
he translated pounds of flesh into emotional demands,
      demands made, demands made.
His application won Frank's praise

but he was living life partially blind.
He tinkered with an idea, a one-may play.
It was small scale theatre
but like an aspirin for the soul,
and when he performed it
- one Friday, Saturday, Sunday -
it gave him back part of himself.

The stage was small, the audience in darkness;
he didn't want to know who was watching him,
there was too much risk in that.
When the applause came
it was like a tonic, a medicine, a salve;
a dosage sufficient to get through Christmas
and the Ambleside anniversary,
to satisfy the bond he had placed upon himself.

Petit Fours

Compact, small - but not petite, not for either gender -
an oval face, almost but not quite round;
short hair, nut brown
- but not brazil (too dark), nor almond (too light) -
neat, uniform ears which remain un-pierced;
lips, in truth, a little on the thin side;
eyes that vary in shade depending on mood.
Nothing to generate remarks or force second glances.
An anonymous image, of stature, of plainness;
a self-imposed loner, a little difficult to process
when failing to conform to common stereotypes.

PJ 'collected' people;   innocent for once,
Mac was to be the jewel in the collection.

When both were hard up and had a little free time
they waited tables in a small dining club;
good food and a Bohemian atmosphere
successfully developing a kind of cache.
On the last lap of March, the weather broke
and people felt released to celebrate Spring;
'The Dining Club', fully booked,
Mac and PJ working harder than ever
in a strangely claustrophobic heat.
After service, Lawrence opened bottles of beer.

"On the house. Why don't you take five outside?"

'Outside': a small secluded courtyard at the back,
forgotten beyond the clatter and steam of the kitchen,
a few plant pots and a sloping patch of lawn.

Mac took a long draught of his beer.
Laid back on the cool grass. Closed his eyes.

One of PJ's hands on his,
lifting it from where it rested on the grass;
lowering it until contact with
warm skin that was not his own.
The sense of a shiver.
Then guided downwards, his fingers found fabric;
guided lower to where it was meant to go.
The slight rise at the crown of the crotch.
The material a little damp.
Fingers brush the material,
a gentle pressure to the body beneath.
Guessing what was expected of him,
press a fraction harder, travel a little further.
PJ's hand raises the edge of her knickers,
guides his fingers again.
The warm and supple folds of her labia;
his fingers, working on their own now,
slowly up and down, in tight little circles,
attuned to the sense her body gave,
gradually increasing the tempo, the pressure.
Fingers moving inside her now.
Urgency as he feels her tense, coiling ready to uncoil.
His fingers moving, in and out,
pressing harder, faster, encouraging her crescendo.

Her body freezes
A small cry.
The release, the relaxation.
Her hand suddenly on his, stilling it.

Mac's eyes still closed,
his hand returned to the coolness of the lawn.
He waits; feels her move, sit up.
He waits, knowing what he wants to happen next -
                            fearing it as much as wishing it.
She stands up.
He hears the chink of a bottle.
He waits, his eyes closed.
And then.
Nothing.

Alone in the courtyard,
eyes open, heart calming,
he takes a pull on his bottle - and waits some more.

Back inside, Laurence oblivious:
"PJ's gone. She said she'll catch you later."

A Fair Exchange

> *I hold the world but as the world, Gratiano,*
> *A stage where every man must play a part,*
> *And mine a sad one.*

shakespeare   you know what to expect don't you
even if you hadn't read   or seen any
almost as if it were gifted   imbued into your psyche
part of your dna   your life force
the quality of mercy   and all that shit

> *Tell me where is fancy bred,*
> *Or in the heart or in the head?*

that was how it felt   suddenly off-balance
side-swiped by an experience that was   well
almost out-of-body   as it were
he struggled   not knowing where this newness
fit in the grand scheme of things   in his history

> *But love is blind, and lovers cannot see*
> *The pretty follies that themselves commit.*

it wasn't as if he'd been   on the lookout
or anything   it wasn't as if he thought himself ready
to go back into battle   to fight for glory
he hadn't forgotten the last war   nor cleared
the battlefield   of all the mines

> *What, wouldst thou have a serpent sting thee twice?*

it was fitting   considering shakespeare and the merchant

that it felt transactional   like a commercial contract
he might have said mercenary   if he'd thought of it
but he didn't   anyway he wasn't ready
to play the romantic   wasn't seeking a portia

    Must I hold a candle to my shames?

she'd known where to find him   in the market of the mind
you might say   a tradesman in others' ideas
librarian of everything   owner of nothing
and if no words were exchanged   as opposed to the silver
in sealing the deal   the arrangement was plain enough

    It blesseth him that gives and him that takes.

it suited them both   she wasn't perfect after all
nor trying to be so   neither did she want any more
than he was prepared to give   that was her gift
releasing him from any bond   not wanting a pound of flesh
just his flesh   and all of it

"They do not move."

Anaesthetised by predictability
he was satisfied not having to think,
Finals just over the horizon.
He was working hard to stand still
dwarfed by effort and the lack of progress.
Echoes returned to him:

> *"Well? Shall we go?"*
> *"Yes, let's go."*
> *They do not move.*

Their regimentation fascinated him,
how PJ ran her life like clockwork
knowing what was coming three days hence.
He had never been enslaved in this way.

Early novelty allowed him flexibility,
the willingness to subjugate himself
as part of a wider experiment;
drawn in as both participant and observer.
The comfort of structure seduced him too,
as if he were granted foreknowledge,
the answers to questions not yet asked.
There was a way she moved, held his hand,
kissed him, made love efficiently;
it was as if everything were ordered,
tidy, not a hair out of place.

> *"We'll come back tomorrow."*
> *"And then the day after tomorrow."*

Then the lack of movement began to gnaw at him,
and he realised movement equalled progress
- enlightenment, even -
but he suffered it, saw it through possessively
even though he had begun to feel like a laboratory specimen,
fed food and drugs to a timetable,
spinning in the little wheel on demand,
his reactions noted somewhere for later analysis.
It was a new type of captivity.

❋

Summer passed in a haze of inactivity
and the inability to make decisions.
He could not work out how he should move on,
or where to, and so he stayed,
around the things he knew, the people he knew;
and though his soul was telling him to fight,
to strike out against the tyranny of the days' blending,
PJ kept him there
smothered by the bliss of certainty.

❋

Then she returned to study
and he awoke
            to nothing.
Anchored by the buoy of their relationship,
he tried to live his old life
as if nothing had happened,
but he was an outsider now;
he was an ex-, deprived of access
to facilities he had taken fore granted.

The world had diverged from him
and looked on him in a new way;
his past had a different status
like a stock that had been downgraded to junk.
He thought of his one-man-show;
now not even valid as a memory.
And what of "Godot"?
Who would remember that?

What else was there that had been tainted?
What else had validity no longer?
He looked at his past via the mirror in his cage
and all the while the world moved on outside.

It was time, he knew, to start making new history.

> *"I thought you were gone forever."*
> *"Me too."*

Release

She saw him struggling
    to come to terms with things;
he was suddenly out of shape
    like a glove with a finger missing.
She had suggested 'The Dining Club'
    though he'd objected,
        said they couldn't afford it.

"Lawrence has given me a special deal."

He should have been worried
    at the divergence;
it didn't fit the way she worked,
    her modus operandi.
He wanted a reason, knowing
    you should never revisit
        the scene of a crime.

After the main course
    he went into the yard for some air.
When he returned
    her chair was empty, bag gone.
Lawrence walked over,
    smiling sadly,
        hand on his shoulder.

"PJ's gone. She said she'll catch you later."

"Act Two"

The Ferryman

It didn't really matter any longer,
life become nothing more than a slow blur,
a film playing on a loop behind a dirty, grey window.
The shapes beyond the glass could have been anyone.
This kind of vagueness they accepted as authentic.
The luxury of ducking questions and massaging truth
small triumphs along the way.

Fog encroaching on the beach,
that was his memory;
an unrelenting tide smoothing and rearranging stones,
dragging them away from him.
He could feel the waves lapping at his feet.

At low water, he found himself in a place
where things were calm,
where he might recall lucidly once again -
and then the tides would turn a moment of strength
into the shabby proof of his weakness.

The Guy most likely to...

Once upon a time he had been unstoppable.
The kind of guy you knew
                      even if you didn't know him.
Always able to pick him out in a crowd,
the guy who seemed to be the focus,
the driving force, the dynamo.
He embraced Pinter and Beckett
        as if they were old drinking pals,
        as if they'd given him the skinny
        on how to wring the best from their words.
Everything he touched was a magnet for applause.
He was the 'guy most likely to'...

And then suddenly you had to check your radar
to see if it was still working, still scanning,
        the 'pings' having gone silent.
The absence of echo was claustrophobic.

Sometimes you'd see him walking around
        alone, like a leper, or
        an animal on the verge of extinction
              no-one wanted to be seen with.
And if you said to someone new
        "See that guy? Man, the things he's done!"
they'd look at you as if you were crazy
        brain-fried from overwork.

People who knew him - vaguely - were left asking
        "what happened after Godot?"
        "what happened in Finals year?"
        "did you hear the rumours about that girl?"

"did he drop out or what,
  the guy most likely to...?"
Maybe a few knew, a small few.
Maybe those who had worked with him
  had the inside scoop.
Maybe a tutor might have let a choice remark slip
  if you'd primed them in the right way;
    Frank was an affable chap after all...
Maybe that girl...
  no, not *that* girl, the other one...

❁

In the end, seeking something inanimate
that could not fight back,
Mac came to believe that 'Art' had let him down;
he felt they'd had a deal, equal shares,
as if he'd been staked in a high-roller game -
  only to find that 'Life' held all the aces,
  the loaded dice, the weighted wheel.
"Just one more spin" he'd said
then found his pockets empty.

He retraced his steps through old books,
wandered their pages like a pilgrim
searching for something he'd dropped along the way.
All he found were cold words,
words he was forced to interpret
through a swirling fog as if they
had been doused in liquid nitrogen
and frozen to the page.
It was a metaphor that primed the need for heat,
and he settled on friction, self-induced,

heat generated by getting moving again;
momentum was everything.
He decided to rub himself up against the world,
to be abrasive, to challenge it.
Railing against fate, the way the cards had fallen,
he became his own guinea pig
measuring and testing
    exposing his reactions to his past.
And obsessed by a sudden notion
    - the 'experience machine'
    that would turn Life into Art -
he cranked the handle
    fuelled the fire
determined to soak up 'being' like a sponge
and turn his self into a living manifesto.

Take no photographs, but be in many

And so he left
> without fanfare
> without a plan
armed with money, a rucksack
and clothing for an indeterminate period.
His mother was nervous
> his father tried to understand;
Jess thought he was crazy
> a kid on the slide
> unstable, ego-centric,
wondering if it would ever be possible
for him to recognise a good thing
> should he come across one again
> (she had loved Mags).

He tried to keep his going low-key
devoid of public expectation;
but inside?
> inside he wanted fanfare and glory again
> either on the journey
> > or in the return.

❁

He hated rules
> but made some,
not to keep him sane
> but to keep him honest
> honest to his purpose
> travelling on his own terms.

1 - No doubling back.
2 - No revisiting -
        of places, people, words.
3 - Do something, move on.
4 - If comfortable, move away.
5 - If sad, angry, lonely, upset, confused
        embrace it, write it down,
        think of the future.
6 - Avoid women who reminded him of
        Mags   Rosie   PJ
        (see rule #2).
7 - Embrace women who reminded him of
        Mags   Rosie   PJ
        (see rule #5).
8 - Train rather than plane;
        bus rather than train;
        walk rather than bus.
9 - Always be reading something new.
10 - Take no photographs
        but be in many.

❊

He zigzagged across Europe and beyond wilfully,
each subsequent destination defined by chance;
        a friend-of-a-friend
        the next train leaving the station
        the roll of a dice
        or the turn of a card.
His progress was haphazard, erratic;
the first few weeks the hardest.
But he was saved by glimpses of beauty -
        Lucca, Sienna, Carcassonne

by the majesty of the historical -
        Athens, Rome, Split.
Gradually he began to see his old self
in the cracked mirrors of run-down hostels,
hear his old voice in bars late at night when
        - too drunk to care -
he recited Shakespeare, Williams, Eugene O'Neill.
He felt like a battery being recharged.
He found people drawn towards him
asking for favours, stories, love;
he worked where he could,
often within the compass of theatre's gravity,
drawn in inexorably.

Sometimes the rules were hard to obey
especially after a triumph.

❁

Investing everything in himself,
he had no time for the tangential;
not going home for his father's funeral nearly broke him
but he wasn't ready
        his project unfinished.
And it was against the rules.
He told himself his father would have understood.

Then one smiling early autumnal day
basking on the shore at Lerici,
thinking of Shelley, and drowning,
he suddenly realised he was empty;
months and months had passed
                and he was spent.

Standing, he stretched towards the bay
and exhaled slowly
      as if blowing his rules into the blue water
          knowing they could not swim.

He picked up his careworn rucksack.

It was time to go home.

Saltburn

She decided she hated the coast,
despising the sly way the snow fell there
making either slush or ice and nothing in between.
Where were those large soft flakes she remembered
from when she was a duffel-coated child,
dropping softly onto the lawn,
the small pond in the back garden,
the big hills white in the distance?
They seemed to bring a reverential silence.
On the coast, snow was mean-spirited
and only brought noise and danger.

Eventually she would leave,
but not really on her own terms
and only after the damage had been done.

Growing up surrounded by structure,
the freedoms of college came as a jolt.
Mac, the yardstick by which she once measured herself,
loosed from constraints and regulations, blossomed;
the exact opposite was true of her.
Not having straight rails to run on,
wandering off a true line was inevitable.
She fell back on the stereotype of 'Jess as Woman':
her features were open and engaging,
and she had a figure that was above passable.
She boasted that "she scrubbed-up well enough".
Mac, on secure ground and self-confident,
was never above berating his older sibling
even if his approach was a little agricultural.

She recalled that Christmas strangely enlivened when
Mac retreated to the Lake District with Mags.
She secretly envied his bravery, the standing up to tradition.
It was what she longed to do
but never found an alternative in which she believed enough.
He had returned for New Year's Eve preoccupied,
and she challenged his slightly off-kilter mood.

"There's a lot going on."

Moving to the coast had been an accident
                                                    - of sorts.
Never as driven as her brother,
she meandered from one redundant job to another;
a meandering much like those country snow falls,
slow and gentle, without any obvious purpose.
In her own way she was experimenting too,
though Mac would bang the brotherly drum
about her letting herself down.
If she knew he was right, she never told him.
It was a vague experimentation that extended
to men and shallow, unrewarding relationships;
a parade of suitors all wrong for her.
Perhaps she hoped one day she would find
the rest of her life magically mapped out.
It was a thin veneer of a philosophy,
embracing Chance as the preferred route into the future.

Those incessant Harpies, Accident and Boredom,
                                                    drove her on;
those and an ever-diminishing faith
that the *next* relationship would be the Motherlode.
It wasn't that she never learned,

but that she consistently failed to apply those learnings.
Tim was a composite of all the knowledge she had acquired
- and all she had ignored;
the acme of what she absolutely did not want or need.

When he arrived unheralded,
Mac was mid-journey 're-finding himself',
trying for size the mask of a new persona:
'Mac-as-traveller'.
The sudden appearance of a tall, slim, charismatic man
was beyond welcome.
Completely undermined by recent disasters,
she embraced the opportunity to be wanted again.
The silent few who loved her but knew *him*
could see she was dropping through a trapdoor.
She thought she was flying,
but was falling and had simply confused the two.

Tim enjoyed making his feelings manifest;
he seduced with imported flowers and fake jewels.
"Tim was selfless" - that was the rose-tinted view.

He landed a lucrative piece of work on the coast.

"Why don't you come with me, Jess?
What have you got to stay here for anyway?"

The first weeks were fine - even with the snow:
a nice flat in a side street near the seafront.
Then one evening Tim returned in a black mood,
a sourness risen to the surface.
Pressing him - what she could do to help? -
she was rebuffed, harshly, instantly.

In the morning he was full of apology
promising dinner out that coming evening

   - a treat that never happened.

Arriving back earlier than usual,
he surprised her as she emerged
having taken a long mid-afternoon bath.
Vaguely dishevelled, tie slightly askew,
his face was tight, host to a darkness in his eyes
she had never seen before.
Expressionless, he stared at her as she stood before him
on the threshold of the bathroom.

"What's wrong? Let me get some clothes on."

He hit her as she turned away,
the blow - a glancing one - unbalanced her.
Before she could move again,
his hands ripped the towel from her body.
The next slap sent her to the floor.
Dazed, he half-lifted, half-dragged her
naked into the bedroom
and threw her onto the freshly-made bed.

She had landed suddenly and painfully,
the trapdoor closing above, cutting off all light.

Departure

Awaking from a sleep she did not recall wanting,
needing, or asking for, she found herself
naked on the bed, the duvet half-pulled over.
Shipwrecked in the kind of quiet
only a permanent separation can bring,
she tried to unpick the silence,
to fill it with something
because silence was the last thing she needed:
the overhead cries of gulls from the beach,
a car going by, a stray voice -
even the rustle of the duvet was welcome.
She swung her feet to the floor.
From somewhere - everywhere - an ache that was new.
Avoiding her reflection in the window,
she could see fragments of Saltburn going about its business,
saw the empty space where Tim would normally park,
heard the echo of a car boot closing,
the tell-tale revving he always gave before moving off
- a sound she would never hear again.

It took her a week to leave.

Her feelings anaesthetised,
recognition of history took some time,
welding herself to the activity
that would protect her in the short-term.
Her approach was calm and methodical,
practical above creative,
ensuring there would be no 'loose ends',
removing any excuse for him to cross her future path.
A desire for extreme separation

prevented her from walking to the police,
showing them her bruises, reporting him for assault.
In making preparations, lists,
she found the courage to face herself in the bathroom mirror.
Was that bruise larger or smaller than she'd expected?
Darker or lighter?
Was she more or less careworn than she had imagined?
Closing this chapter as clinically as she could,
was the chance for her to undertake a purge,
a personal cleansing;
if an item possessed an unbreakable mental link to him
then it was gone, thrown into anonymous black bin-liners
and sealed with as hard a knot as she could muster.
She was surprised just how much had been tainted.

Posting her set of keys through the letter box,
just two bags accompanied her to the railway station.

The Garden Bench

In one sense, she had never really 'left'.
She flitted butterfly-like, trying to find somewhere to settle.
Occasionally she would appear at home again to take refuge,
awaiting the promise of another opportunity.

Tim was the shortest interlude of all.

Afterwards, she slotted seamlessly back into the old house,
the essence of their family resolutely entrenched,
the remnants of her old life persistently intact.
The most notable thing that was different
was her mother's slight distance,
as if there were an unseen obstruction in the way.

"There's something. Is it me?"

Jess had refrained from telling them whole story,
wondered if her concealment was that transparent.

"Don't say you haven't noticed?"

The man who had opened the door to her,
who had made her tea,
who had sat across from her at dinner,
who looked a little tired and had lost some weight -
her father was dying.

She replayed the conversation with her mother
in the solitude of her old room,
surrounded by things her mother had refused to throw away
knowing that cherished things from childhood

never become un-cherished;
that the passing of time overlays a veneer of mythology
to make them even more precious.
The word 'terminal' had not been uttered
though the projected outcome was clear;
any treatment would be unpleasant
with little prospect of a positive impact.

"Why put myself - put you - through such agony?
There are no miracles."

They had spent their life making the best of things, he said.

"He doesn't want a fuss. Isn't that typically him?"

All the time *he* could manage,
that's exactly what *they* would do.
Jess wondered how they might define 'manage',
and from whose perspective.
She assumed they would muddle on,
like they always did.
It felt like a family heirloom.

"He has asked me to ask you *not* to talk to him about it.
He wants things to be normal for as long as possible."

"What about Mac? Have you told him?"

Her mother offered a small smile,
resignation and failed understanding smuggled into it.

"It's difficult to tell him anything
when you don't know where he is.

I'm sure he'll come home when he's good and ready,"

Jess suspected her father might be less forgiving.
For her, Mac was selfish in the extreme;
there was only one place he needed to be.

"Why didn't you tell me until now?
I've not been in bloody Romania!"

"You were having your own struggles weren't you?
It seemed as if things might be turning around.
You seemed optimistic. We didn't want to damage that."

Outside in the well-loved garden,
tucked away in an alcove, a wooden bench
and an uninterrupted view along the garden's length.
Jess sat in the spring chill and cradled a warm mug;
she heard the back door latch,
watched as her father made his way
towards the fraying shed.
Unaware she was spying,
he moved less fluently than of old,
slightly stooped, his pace compromised.
He walked as if he were a man burdened.
She cursed herself for being selfish,
yet still wasn't ready for a conversation with him.
There were things she needed to process first.

As she struggled to re-orient her life,
the garden bench became the outpost
from which she tried to chart her future -
and marked her father's decline.
Sometimes he would catch her looking after him.

"I know you're there", he said once over his shoulder
off on an errand to retrieve herbs from the vegetable patch.
And all the while - as her father became slower
and more stooped, thinner and paler -
she waited to hear from Mac.
Jess imagined her parents
        - their parents -
insulated somehow,
inoculated against fear or disappointment.

As she sat on her bench, it came to feel
as if there were a fourth person living in the house;
an invisible spectre who was haunting them all,
and haunting them in different ways.

Jess hadn't seen the end coming;
hadn't anticipated the swiftness of it.
One day, her father had simply said -

"Let's cut to the chase".

His collapse was strangely without theatre;
he had always been able to remove drama from a situation.
She wondered if he had become some kind of philosopher -
or perhaps he had always been one
and she had failed to recognise it.
Two days after he had been admitted Mac called,
her mother casually mentioning it
as the two of them sat eating supper,
both trying not to look at the empty chair across from them.

"And did you tell him?"

Unable to rise to her bait,
Jess realised that her mother was simply exhausted;
so washed out she had no more capacity for feeling.

"He was definitely tired, I could tell that."

"Aren't we all?"

"He said he'd ring again when he got to where he was going.
To see how things were."

"I just don't understand what he's waiting for!"

"I don't think you've ever understood him, have you dear?
I'm not sure any of us have.
Except your father, perhaps.
They are more alike than you probably realise."

No longer the smell of small miracles

Supposed to be antiseptic white
the ward had a tone about it, shadowed
by the years of comings and goings
as if each unimportant journey
left something of the traveller behind.
In spite of the off-ness of its colour
- or the colour it possessed
where there should have been none -
if smelled just as it should:
>harsh white linens
>ointments
>discarded newspapers
>old coffee cups
>new flowers in new water
>old flowers in old
>bandages
>cleanliness.

For most it was the smell of endeavour,
of hope, of luck, of trust;
it was the smell of small miracles.

For Jess, staring at the unmade bed,
it was the smell of death.

Knowing her father had made his contribution
to defeat the whiteness of the room,
she picked up his shallow little bag
>>>and left.

For the Love of Daffodils

Expecting tradition,
expecting a smothering of black,
    of sorrowful faces,
expecting the epitome of dirge
    (whatever that meant)
she was surprised by how people smiled,
by how vibrant they looked.
Everywhere was yellow and orange and white.
It had been his request,
to remind him of his garden;   he said,
people should dress as if he were there
    and to celebrate daffodils
        his favourite flower.

She had never known that.

They had entered serenaded by Cat Stevens, of all people:

> *"It's not time to make a change,*
> *just relax, take it easy,*
> *you're still young*
> *that's your fault,*
> *there's so much you have to know."*

'Father and Son', a song for both the Absent and her.

She cried.

> *"I was once like you are now,*
> *and I know that it's not easy,*
> *to be calm when you've found*

something going on."

At the lectern, sharp and clean as if it were
designed for a business conference,
a man in a suit went through the motions,
reading his script, talking to the delegates
about a man he didn't know.

For a moment she was angry.

Then another man, her father's age,
dark suit, white hair, bright yellow tie, stood up,
standing to the side as if not wishing to intrude,
knowing he was a supporting act.
He looked at them,
                at the heavy coffin,
and betrayed by his red eyes,
looked down at the sheet of paper
shaking in his hands, and said

      "I have a message from Douglas."

❊

You all look lovely.   It's like spring has sprung all over again! Thank you.   I wish I could be there with you - though I am of course, in a manner of speaking.   Did they play the Cat Stevens?   Something for Mac and Jess, though not very original, I admit.   I hope you made it back, Mac.   If not, know that I'm thinking about you - which I realise is a little bit the wrong way round, but there you have it.   Our lives encapsulated.   If I were a religious man - no, that's wrong. If I were a 'believer' then I'd make some smug comment about being on 'the last journey', knowing that there is one final, glorious, never-ending tour stop where the gin-and-tonic never runs out and Chantilly cream and pickled onions are banished; a wonderful venue for a sunset, even if no postcards are allowed! But I'm not, and so - with due regard to my few believer friends - I know I'm not going anywhere any more. At least not consciously. Which is actually fine, isn't it? Inevitable, but fine. I've had, as they say, a fair crack at it; Life. There are some things I am proud of, most of which are, in one way or another, represented by the people here today. Look around. Smile. If anything, remember that each one of you here is part of my story, made up part of my story. Made me. So don't let that part of you, or anything I had to do with *your* story, slip into the fiery furnace. Never let those things go. They are precious, unique, ours. I gift them to you, for you to keep, to look after. Treasure them. Please.

❃

After, people bequeathed stories of his humour, his honesty,
the practical jokes he played when he was younger.
There were tales of bravery too.
She hadn't known he had rescued a boy from drowning,
diving into the Avon fully clothed
downstream from Worcester.

"He didn't like to boast about it" her mother said.

And she wondered how much folklore
had been lost to her through his modesty;
and she wondered how much she knew him after all.
Replaying the song in her head -

> *"All the times that I've cried*
> *keeping all the things I knew inside*
> *it's hard, but it's harder to ignore it."*

- she cried again.

Returning Home

The entrance was always a little grand for the house.
At this time of day, at this time of year,
the light shining above the heads of those
who might be coming or going
glowed more yellow than usual,
a tone inherited from the stone door-frame
and the ageing bulb.
It was the tint clouds possess
when there is snow in the offing,
both promising and threatening.
A house at one with nature?
A bellwether for the state of things?
To him, as familiar as any house could be,
its aura told you everything you needed to know.
From the street-side of the gate,
the tall hedge that protected the house
framed the frame of the door.
His father had hated that hedge with a vengeance;
even so, perhaps the hedge would miss him too.

Hesitant, he decided to knock.
It seemed appropriate to wait, to be admitted.
What would have surprised them?
What might have caused a catching of the breath?
If he had not turned up alone;
that would have been something!
A ghost resurrected from his past
or the spectral promise of a different future…
The door opened and the hall's bright light flooded out
to relegate that wistful yellow glow to memory.
"I've just made coffee" was what she said,

taking him in, all in one swift glance;
he had conveyed so much just by standing there.
He dropped his bag and looked around;
the same paintings hung on the walls,
the same slightly bloomed mirror.
Why should those have changed?
Who was going to set the tone now?
In darkness, a room, his father's bolthole,
a means of escape above all else.
Detached, in another, his mother
upright in her old wing-back chair
staring at a television years out of date and
turned up so loud it made his ears hurt.
Remotely, he dropped the sound by half;
she looked round, confused, then up at him.

"Michael! I didn't hear you come in".

He intercepted her with a strange half-hug
then she sank back into the chair;
behind her, Jess, a coffee cup in each hand.
There was more than enough in her stoney look.
She too had been through much;
he hadn't been there for her either.

"Yes. Sorry I'm a bit late."

Jess' boundaries of lateness were defined
by his not coming home when their father died,
leaving her to ease her mother's burden;
the organiser, the shoulder to cry on, the practical head.

He had only been there five minutes

but felt his optimism ebbing away.

"How's London?"

"Just a landing point before coming up here."

"Landing from where - exactly?"

His mother used to test him on flags and capital cities,
always trying to catch him out;
a childhood experience that had given him a 'bucket list'.
He had ticked off so many in the last three years.

"Italy? Is that where you were two months ago?"

Jess wanted to land a fierce uppercut,
but all she could do was jab, jab.
There would be another round, he knew.

"I was probably in Mombassa in September."

"Probably?" Jab, jab.

"Drink your coffee, Dear, before it gets cold.
They make coffee in Kenya, don't they?"

He picked up his coffee.
It was already too cool for him.

"I heard"

Slicing through the silence of the house, the phone.
Sitting in his room, trying to sift through
his legacy there and the detritus of his journey,
he felt like an Archaeologist
rearranging the pieces until they made sense,
wishing for a find of unspeakable treasure.

Jess' voice, friendly, welcoming,
ascended the stairs two at a time
though he couldn't see why.
She chatted; an old friend, obviously.
Then, unexpectedly:

"Mac, it's for you!"

*

"Hello Mac."

Her voice transported him seamlessly
across years and counties until he was deposited again
in a small terraced cottage in Ambleside.
He glanced out of the window
to check the weather, to reorient.

"Mags…"

"I heard about your father.
I heard about Jess.
I heard you were back.
I just wanted to say sorry."

Flooded with questions about knowledge
and how it was gathered, discovered,
found, uncovered, garnered,
his first emotion could only be of guilt.

"Yes," he said, to cover all options.
And, "Thanks."

"I wanted to come to the funeral,
he was such a lovely man.
Jess said it was wonderful in its own sad way;
people celebrating, not mourning.
Not so much.
But I didn't go.
I didn't see how I could, without you there.
And if you had been, not knowing
if you'd want me to."

The earpiece was cold against his skin,
and as she spoke he felt something drain from him.
Unable to identify it
         he could only feel it;
and only able to feel it, it felt like loss,
like losing everything he had ever known;
it felt as if he was being robbed of something profound
even as he stood there, complicit in the crime.

"Yes. Of course. You would have been welcome."

"Is your mother okay?" she asked,
the last word meaning nothing
yet layered with a depth only context can bring.

He thought of her now,
sitting in the kitchen peeling - something -
radio on too loud, a little more forgetful;
recalled the glances passed between him and Jess
across the dinner table, the living room,
knowing she missed her husband more than she could say;
sliding inexorably and rapidly towards him.
So soon.

"Coping, just."

His lie clogged on the line,
from somewhere a crackle as if objection were being made.

"Sorry, I lost you there" came her voice
as the stillness returned.

Feeling broken and defeated
as if he had been wrung out,
squeezed through a mangle,
he wondered what more there was to say.
He left it to her
           just as he always used to.

"Look. I was wondering.
I'd understand if not.
Whether you wanted a drink.
Sometime.
For old times' sake.
Just to catch up."

Decline, the white flag

If somewhere a butterfly flapped its wings
- perhaps even there, in their garden,
white or brilliant blue dancing between tired daffodils -
then she failed to see it
as much as she failed to hear
      the oncoming tsunami.

Forlorn, sound retreated;
the radio and television ceased to work,
their silence wordlessly celebrated
in the dumb lights on the tuning dial
and by open-mouthed actors
      who said nothing any more.

Striped of their identities,
things became abstracts of themselves
abandoning the rulebook;
salt in the tea, sugar in the rice.
What did it matter any more
      if the spice was gone from life?

One day, preparing something irrelevant,
she watched the small red pool grow
glistening bright on the tablecloth,
her essence pouring from the finger
that had inadvertently strayed into the path
      of a paring knife.

And strangers, fussing constantly about,
him and her, feigning friendliness,
mouthing, making gestures,

as if *she* needed to be a part of *their* urgency.

There was no dignity in her decline,
the white flag waving.

The harder they tried
       the more she resisted
              subsumed by an unwavering focus

                      on a horizon they could not see.

"What next?"

Dark, sombre, devoid of eulogy,
the day washed over them,
a harsh tide on a pebble-strewn beach
sucking them all towards the void
even as they stood, and trembled,
                                and sang.

It was the negative from a colour print;
in black and white and grey
the alternative perspective.
They tried to celebrate her
but there were no tales of heroism,
no great waves of humour;
they tried to rejoice but found emptiness.

Jess wanted to believe in her mother,
that there was more to her life
than a semi-empty casket;
she wanted to believe that one day
they would uncover a treasure trove of memories
buried in the dust-enamelled attic
abandoned since her father's passing.

When they had taken sides
it had always been Boys versus Girls.
She liked to recall the Girls' supremacy,
but standing on the damp and flattened grass
her eyes stone-bound
she wondered if that were true at all,
if Mac's loyalties hadn't been more shrewdly placed.
She could see in him an image of their father.

Solid, upright, slightly detached,
he addressed the day professionally,
ensuring process and timing, starving emotion.
He became a pillar for her to lean on
- which she did more than once,
though never really understanding why.

"Do you remember", he said,
"that holiday in the Lakes when Dad and I
threw stones into Buttermere for nearly an hour
and you and Mum refused to join in?"

Even then it was a memory of *him*;
even at his wife's funeral,
their father came to the fore.
So unlike life!

❁

Silent, side-by-side yet miles apart
they rode in the gloss-black car
       back to the house.
It was theirs now,
       even the empty spaces
       the favourite chairs
       the outmoded crockery.

When they entered, the house asked
       "what next?"
so they walked into the garden,
Jess returning to her bench
watching Mac losing himself among
the raised beds he had been trying to tend,

the daffodils long gone over.
Behind her, the house again
         "what next?"

As if hearing the question,
Mac stopped and looked back towards her.
He tried to smile
- not for him but for her -
but the smile got lost beyond the herbs.

"What next?" said the house
the shed, the brazier, all the old tools,
the tubers and bulbs, the wilting leaves.

Everything asked him the same question
- for Mags had been at the funeral.

Interlocking

When she took his hand
it was as if he were feeling her fingers for the first time,
as if he had been given an unexpected present,
coming without fanfare, without wrapping.
Without ceremony
        it was suddenly there.

Love sought is good, but given unsought, is better.

They looked at their entwined hands
as if together they had become a separate being
the rest of them along for the ride,
voyeurs for whatever the hands decided to do.

Good pilgrim, you do wrong your hand too much,
which mannerly devotion shows in this;
For saints have hands that pilgrims' hands do touch,
And palm to palm is holy palmers' kiss.

He lifted hers to his lips and kissed the back of it;
an archaic gesture, like an old priest's blessing.

When thou dost ask me blessing, I'll kneel down
And ask of thee forgiveness.

"So" she said
        shivering her nervousness away.

And flooding back came echoes
of comfort, warmth,
    of solidity, security,

                of toast,
the drawing back of curtains to admit light
onto an old past,
        one that was good
                where nostalgia was permitted.

But this was not the old past.
It was a new beginning that one day would graduate
to be another past, another iteration.
How might he want to look back on this one
        when the time came?

        Maybe all one can do is hope to end up with the right regrets.

Mags had rules of her own
spelled out in some secret silent morse
transmitted through her fingers' squeeze
that only he could understand:
        no discussing the past,
        no wavering,
        only look forwards,
        be creative
                in this new world
                        together.

    Out of my lean and low ability
    I'll lend you something.

He knew what kind of chance this was,
        a second chance
        a final chance.
Jess had cried when he told her.

"Don't fuck it up this time…"

Her words,
> but he heard his voice in them too.

"We should go away," he suggested,
his next words to her
committing to everything she had said
when she silently took his hand.

"We should go away," she replied,
as if she were sealing the deal,
counter-signing on the dotted line.

> *We are not the first*
> *Who, with best meaning, have incurr'd the worst.*

"I've already booked the cottage in Ambleside.
In two weeks.
We can have Christmas again…"

He looked up at the October clouds
scudding as they always must
like businessmen rushing
> late as usual
>> for their next important meeting,
dragging dead leaves and rain behind them,
the dour Ambassadors for winter.

"Christmas come early," he said,

> and they walked on.

"Act Three"

Choice

Sometimes there is a choice.
Not stark or binary, like heads or tails
where outcomes are known
        even if their consequences are not;
but subtle, nuanced,
flavoured like the addition of herbs and spices
to raw ingredients,
the Magician's trick to serve up
Italian, or French, or Asian.
The essence is not in 'yes' or 'no'
but how the judgement is delivered, embellished,
the tone of voice, the careful wrapping of an answer
bound in patterned paper,
tied by a ribbon that has been teased
until it curls professionally.

Or not.

Not because there is no smoothing,
no way or need to coat the pill;
but because - beyond the camouflage of self-deceit -
the choice remains yes or no, heads or tails,
its core undeniable, its ripples
on an infinite journey to unseen shores.

Old Shoots, New Leaves

They spent what little spare money they had
on flat-pack bookcases, white
not to detract from the spines,
individual splashes of colour conspiring
to make a statement
        a compound of them together.
Some things they kept separate,
a private parcel of their intellectual lands,
        - the blend was of novels and poetry,
        plays and history books apart -
boundaries less robust than a dry stone wall
        yet just as definitive.

They nibbled at careers
teasing their way through life one strand at a time,
keeping to shortened horizons
        invisible checkpoints.
At the end of each month
they would treat themselves to a meal out
or a take-away from the up-market Indian,
the gradually increasing pile of rinsed-out cartons
providing their own testimony:
        "made it this far".
They were tasting life together again,
remembering spices and subtle seasonings,
what worked and what did not,
as if they were engaged in research
for the ultimate cook book,
        a recipe of secrets.

And in the spaces they created for each other

Mags tried to remind herself how to draw,
        to knit, to sew;
Mac began writing again -
"One line at a time" he said, then later
        "Act One, Scene Two."
If it were a double-hander
he lived in fear of the third character
appearing out of nowhere,
        the Villain, the Motley Fool,
        the Jackanapes,
            the Temptress.
The spectre of Beckett never left him;
he steered clear of the minimal.

And all the while, in the wings as it were,
Jess looked on, buoyed by Mags' smile,
her low-level radiation of contentment.
She watched as they re-learned how to move
together, around each other, apart,
like an old clockwork toy whose key had been found
        and its parts oiled.
Imperceptibly they wound the spring,
        kept the engine running.
And if the house were asking "What next?"
it did so in a lower register,
more a whisper now;
and seeing Mac reborn
she stopped fearing the answer.

They talked about the house, about selling it;
they talked about the money
discussing over red wine and pizza
all the things they could do with it.

But they weren't ready to move beyond
        the hypothetical,
so they lived in it - the three of them -
breathing life and colour into the place,
gradually rewarding it for its service;
a new carpet here,
                or a lick of paint.
A new bulb for the porch light.

And Mac learned how not to kill
the herbs and vegetables,
and during springtime
        there were always daffodils.

As the garden flourished
Jess learned how not to hate her brother,
to love how together they talked about her
sitting side-by-side on the garden bench
Mags luxuriating in the bath upstairs
listening to the murmur of their voices
as it climbed the ivy
and snuck in through the bathroom window
        left ajar for just that purpose.

Eventually "what next?" would evaporate
whisked away on the slenderest breeze,
a fragment of memory
        nothing more.
And one day Jess stopped looking beyond,
        beyond the house
        beyond the money
        beyond the garden
        beyond tomorrow

   because she was happy with all of them.

It was as if her family had been enriched
by all that was good in Mags,
her bravery and tolerance above all things.
She grew into the sister Jess had never had,
the confidant she had always needed;
gradually the disappointment she felt in herself
for believing in a mother who did not exist
that vanished too
   involuntary, invisible
      lost with "what next?"

They started to learn what 'enough' meant,
the brother and sister who had chased the illusive
   the impossible
      the ideal.

The Coniston Question

"Do you love me?"

Smoke from 'The Gondola' whipped into the air,
dissipated into nothing.
The wind stole conversations,
        dragged words from sentences
and threw them overboard
to leave them at the mercy of the choppy waters.
Clouds bullied,
        the brilliance of the land becoming muted;
clouds like thieves feasting on colour.

She knew he had heard her perfectly.

"Do you love me?"

Under a sudden shadow
the funnel's gold lost its gleam and sparkle.
It felt like a measure of something profound.

The people sitting closest to him
seemed unperturbed by her question.
He knew precisely what it meant,
as if she were testing the temperature,
knowing his answer could throw up different scenarios:
        hand-in-hand or not, smiling or not,
        kissing tenderly or not,
        taking coffee and cake in the cafe
            - or not.
Her one question spawned
an unfathomable number of others.

Had it spilled out on the spur of the moment
or had she been struggling with it for days
knowing it could never be a question without consequence?
Momentarily he was trapped;
    trapped by the limited space,
        the ship's rails,
            the water, the clouds,
                even the land itself.

Perhaps two seconds had passed.

'No'

For the merest of moments
>   less than a blink
>   shorter than a shutter click

Mac had held the answer 'no' on his lips
and weighed how heavy it felt,
how it tasted of all those things
he had hated since a child:
>   cough syrup
>   peanut butter
>   kippers
>   celeriac.

Then with a breath it was gone
scudding across the water,
>   invisible,
>   banished,

heading for the shore to be picked up
by someone else, perhaps polished,
burnished in such a way
>   as to make it feel like not 'no'.

It was right that person was not him.

'Yes'

"Struggling to admit fool mistakes once made
and severed from clear headedness, I'd tend
to seek the deepest most reclusive shade
and hide myself within, afraid to lend
much hope against a world so counterfeit.

How could I know I would be saved by you?

"With my compass found and once more reset
I now recast my future self anew,
shake off the torments of those bleakest years
and in embracing life attempt to show
how recharged through your love I must appear,
rejoicing afresh in all that I know,

"and - 'Yes' - not to withhold a single part
from the bounteous mercy of your heart."

If there was a difference...

If there was a difference they could not name it
yet saw it manifest in the frivolous:
    plans for things to do or where to go,
    new kitchen utensils,
    a bucket-list filled with impossibilities,
    watercolours at last honouring their subject,
    words that sounded, finally
            as if they needed to be spoken.

They edged towards a less nervous future.
Mac celebrating with his father's garden
growing carrots for the first time;
Mags rescuing cookery books and finding
a love of bread and a knack for jam.
Together they plotted raspberries
and a tiny orchard
         of apple, pear and damson.

Slowly they began to unwrap the past,
Jess and Mac, closeted on the garden bench,
speaking of their parents, unburdening
their memories, what they had felt,
delicately comparing notes as if fragile-edged
and building a collage from the images left behind
to frame and put away
            somewhere safe.

Skins

I watch them as they dance through life
like some practiced married couple
moulding themselves to fit each other.

Then, from somewhere in our previous life
his vitriol returns to me;
how she bullied him to prove superiority,
how she always told on him
        and could never keep a secret.

Different people for different times,
shedding skins as we mature.

I too shed a skin back then.
If you should find it, lying uselessly about,
you might recognise it by the pattern
and its blemishes,
        uneven ugly shapes,
the brown and blue of a battered heart.

I lie.

I keep it still in a nondescript cardboard box.
From time to time I take it out,
examine it beneath a kinder light.
The bruises have a lustre
as if there were beauty in them,
as if they had to be earned, scars of battle,
to get me where I am today -
watching them dance in our kitchen
        my sleeves rolled up, the burgeoning smells

of raspberry jam coming from the bubbling pot.

❀

This day is different.
This day it is my turn to fit to Jess,
to pretend that we are family
    though how much closer could we be
    after all these happy years?

The three of us.

Today Jess needs to tell me
    what she can't tell him;
the reason she dropped that serving dish
all those months ago, and why
she takes a little longer in the bathroom
    or climbing the stairs,
why she only carries one plate at a time
and prefers to get a taxi back from town.

I have watched her and I know
    before she speaks.
I have watched him and I know
    he has no idea.

If this day is hard
    for her, for me,
tomorrow will be hardest for Mac
when she takes him tea in the garden
and they sit on the bench
and she explains why her bucket list
needs to be a little shorter

      and a little more important.

He will cry.

And I will wait inside the house
cradling my little cardboard box.
There's room enough in there
to add the bruised skin he will slough,
      the scars of living.

As if nothing had happened

Neglecting the garden for a few days
felt like a protest
        though it wasn't really.
He needed to rail against unfairness;
he wanted to kick and shout and scream
but he was too old for that now
and the neighbours would have objected
or called the police, fearing wrongdoing.

Which it was
        in a way.

He watched her incessantly now,
seeking out the nuance in each move,
watching her turn of phrase
      - his turn of phrase -
daunted by the peril of a word out of place.
And it seemed as if it were only he
who was upset, angry,
Jess and Mags carrying on as if
nothing had happened
      even though it had
           and somehow a long while ago.

Returning to the garden
he tended the earth with greater focus
as if being a better gardener would make a difference.
He was thinking of Jess
      but of himself too;
dead-heading roses, thinning seedlings,
      symbols for him tending his own life.

Leaning on his fork, he stood,
straightening a back that was less reliable these days
and saw them through the kitchen window.
For a moment he was his father
watching Jess and his mother there.
Had *he* been as much in awe?

He remembered coming back from Europe,
walking into Jess' hostility;
        she had been merciless then
- and he knew now she had been right.

They had never truly recovered until Mags returned
knitting them all together in her quiet way.

Returning to the fork, he shook his head.
Now look at them!
Now look at what Mags had grown.
In truth the apples, pears, damsons were all hers,
he was just the instrument;
and even the peace between he and Jess
a concord renewed without question day by day
        had been her doing.

He watched her too
        and could only marvel.

The Sculptor of Life

At certain times of the year
        at certain times of the day
the sun would hang low
over the far corner of the garden   and pause
as if in melancholic reflection,
sending spears of light through the kitchen window.
Looking out
    a halo spread
to edge the laurel, the shed, in sunset yellow;
and Mac - as she saw him now,
bent to the protection of his crop -
become a darkened shadow of himself
outlined by something ethereal
                        almost heavenly.

He was never heavenly, she knew that;
not even now,
    not even as he strived to fight time,
the time that leaked away from her.

Never spiritual,
    recently she had forsaken fiction
for theories about life and living,
some - said Mac - as much fiction as fiction…
And Mags had laughed
    fingering the books noncommittally.

She used to think there came a point beyond which
life was all about decay, the cruelest joke
that you never knew the tipping point
until it was too late, already succumbing

                                    to the fall.
But someone said there was no decay;
that living was all about being shaped
         day after day
to become the thing you were meant to be.
She imagined herself
         born a block of marble
the Sculptor of Life chipping away incessantly
getting ever closer to what it was
                            she should be.

She still hadn't lost her taste for the romantic!

That sun setting, Mac's surreal outline,
Mags' marvellous Bakewell Tart,
         the struggle in the shops today:
chip, chip, chipping away.
She wondered what would remain,
feeling as if she had so little left to give,
         as if she might be sculpted to nothing.

Perhaps that was it;
         you woke up one day
                   and you weren't there any more.

She wanted to be angry
but found herself spent by past endeavours.
She had used up her stock of anger it seemed
         - on Tim,
                   on Mac,
                            herself -
and she was glad.

She was too tired to be angry.

Staring down the garden, into that melancholic sun,
she felt just a little recharged,
as if she had been given something back
       something with which to fight
              the incessant chisel.

Smiling at the illusion,
she knew tomorrow would be the same,
each day diminishing
       until she became what she was meant to be.

After the Rehearsals

He remembered the feeling
                    after the rehearsals:
the arrival of opening night;
                    the nervousness of butterflies;
the rumbling of the settling audience
                    always louder than expected.
Then silence began to descend
                    triggered by nothing
but some psychic anticipation
                    that the lights were about to dim.

At the hospital, sound had faded out too;
first the chatting, then the murmuring,
the pulse beat of the machines.

On the stage he knew what to do with silence;
he knew how to fill it with his exuberance or passion;
knew how to take control with words,
                  how to fill the void.
But not there.
Not where murmuring had moved from room to corridor,
where the beeping of machines came from the wings.

✤

Beneath a chill sky that belied all seasons,
        they gathered again.
Music came from the leaves in the trees,
the birds, the dull roar of the highway;
then from a synthesised organ, recorded,
piped into the crucible where they had gathered.

And even though it was like a stage,
and even though they hushed on cue,
and even as he stood to take his turn,
to play his part - Best Supporting Actor -
he was bereft in so many ways.

He looked out at a sea of faces,
                             and not for the first time
there were tears in those eyes,
                             and he was reminded - of all things -
of Godot…

        "Well? Shall we go?"
        "Yes, let's go."
        They do not move.

Clearing his throat, he searched for his lines
eventually allowing instinct to take over,
trusting one of the few things he had left
now that Jess was gone.

Mags smiled weakly at him.

It was time.

"It is, these dark days, something of a modern tradition
to read verse, a poem, on such dark occasions,
as if the words of others can do the job so much better;
as if those who never knew - you, Jess -
can describe what I am feeling.
                             Right here.
                             Right now.

"I don't know.

"I tried myself, of course.

"I used to write things and try them out on you,
and with your sharp wit you'd dismiss the weak
with a scathing assessment of 'just crap, Mac'.
                              [laughter, a little]
Anything you liked - even moderately - fared little better.
                              [laughter, softly]
If you said something was 'okay', I knew I'd hit the jackpot."

It was funny how he could hear the tears
even as he heard the laughter.
Perhaps it was like Godot, after all.

"In a play that is part of my soul, a character says
        "I thought you were gone forever."
and the reply comes back
        "Me too.".
But of course this time you are gone forever, Jess.
I could say my line, but never hear it batted back.

"I do not know how you can encapsulate
                    what that's like in words.
I do not know how words can possibly suffice
                    to bridge such an awful gap.
And words have been my life.
Words, and the house, our life together, us three.
All a little less whole now, less adequate.

"This is all I have left, all my inadequacy can offer;
a meagre tribute, knowing that even a lifetime

spent in drafting just a single line would prove insufficient to say what needs to be said.

> "Be comforted that you are in our mind,
> that thoughts of you are always swathed in love,
> that ne'er will our memory weakness find,
> your presence here never by force removed.
>
> "Rest easy knowing you have made your mark;
> foundations laid, resolute, unshaken.
> Protected as are trees by their stout bark,
> so is your name safe, whole, unforsaken.
>
> "If today we loose tears upon our cheeks,
> in part it's fearing that demesne to come;
> ahead our solitude in future weeks
> seen this dark day, our mourning and our doom.
>
> "Rest comforted today as thus is proved
> with warmth and truth and heart that you were loved."

The Library

Sometimes in the bleakness
I see myself walking into the void of memory
hunting for something I know once was there.
It is a colourless place, devoid of dimensions,
and though I cannot tell up from down
        nor left from right,
I outstretch a metaphorical hand
still hoping to grasp that which I seek:
a name, a place, a fragment playing
        on a never-ending loop
            always ready.

Too often I leave empty handed, like
a fisherman who had forgotten to bait the hook, or
whose lures are frightening the fish.
Pause.   Flex the line.   Re-cast.
Definition of lunacy: doing the same thing again,
        expecting a different result.

Sometimes I surprise myself
- now travelling without expectation -
to feel something in my grasp
even if it is the wrong answer.
David, Daniel, Derek;
might as well be all the same.

When I get it right I can tell by their faces,
the sudden unrestrained smiles.
Is that what victory feels like, I can't recall?
And when I'm wrong, they nod appreciatively
as if I've done them a favour,

as if it was all in the trying;
"better luck next time".

Which, let's face it,
                is bollocks, really.

I had a moment the other day
- or it may have been this morning,
    it hardly matters -
a moment when I was greeted
not by formless nothingness
but by a light-flooded library,
rows and rows of books
their luminous spines arranged
in whatever order I wanted.

I remembered so many things
in that one brief visit;
        cottages in the Lake District,
        adventures in foreign places,
        being blinded by footlights,
        the thrill of a keyboard,
        and daffodils, and carrots,
        the flowers of an orchard...

And Jess was there, of course.
I had forgotten how much I missed her
even though somewhere, sometime,
                I swore that I would not.

I cried.

Later, after the light had faded

and I was hauled back to wherever this place is,
to be fussed over, poked and prodded,
made singularly uncomfortable for no good reason,
I noticed a face amid blue uniformed faces.
It was a face that belonged in my library.

I smiled, hopefully.

The face cried.

*

Acknowledgements

Excerpts and quotations:
- "As You Like It", William Shakespeare; Signet Classic (The New American Library of World Literature Inc.), 1963
- "King Lear", William Shakespeare; New Penguin Shakespeare (Penguin Books), 1972 (1978 reprint used)
- "The Merchant of Venice", William Shakespeare; Signet Classic (The New American Library of World Literature Inc.), 1965
- "The Ride Down Mount Morgan", Arthur Miller; premier in London, 1991 (quote taken from wikiquote, en.wikiquote.org/wiki/Arthur_Miller)
- "Romeo and Juliet", William Shakespeare; Airmont Shakespeare Classic Series (Airmont Publishing Company Inc.), 1966
- "The Sonnets", William Shakespeare; Signet Classic (The New American Library of World Literature Inc.), 1965
- "Father and Son" from "Tea for the Tillerman", Cat Stevens; Island Records, 1970
- "Waiting for Godot", Samuel Beckett; Faber and Faber, 1956 (1977 reprint used)

www.ingramcontent.com/pod-product-compliance
Lightning Source LLC
Chambersburg PA
CBHW030528080526
44586CB00011B/366